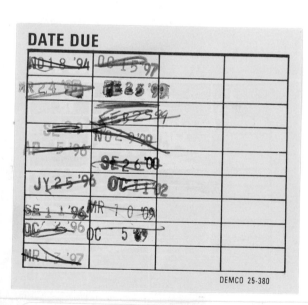

SLIDE GUITAR

•

A BOOK/RECORD GUIDE TO ELECTRIC LEAD
AND TRADITIONAL SLIDE AND BOTTLENECK STYLES

•

WITH SPECIAL CHAPTERS ON
IMPROVISING BLUES
AND COUNTRY & WESTERN LEAD GUITAR

•

PLUS A RIFF ON OPEN TUNINGS

•

**By the Staff of
Green Note Music Publications**

SCHIRMER BOOKS
A Division of Macmillan Publishing Co., Inc.
NEW YORK

Collier Macmillan Publishers
London

Schirmer Books, A Division of Macmillan Publishing Co., Inc.
866 Third Avenue, New York, New York 10022
Collier-Macmillan Canada Limited.

Printed in the United States of America.

This edition published under agreement with
Green Note Music Publications, Inc.

Exclusive publisher to the Music Trade:

Green Note Music Publications
P. O. Box 4187
Berkeley, California 94704

Library of Congress Catalog Number: 72-76529
International Standard Book Number: 0-912910-02-X

SLIDE GUITAR

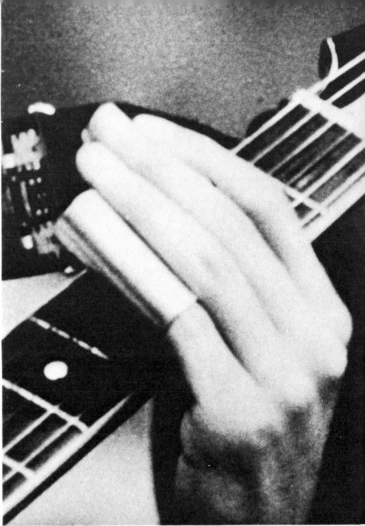
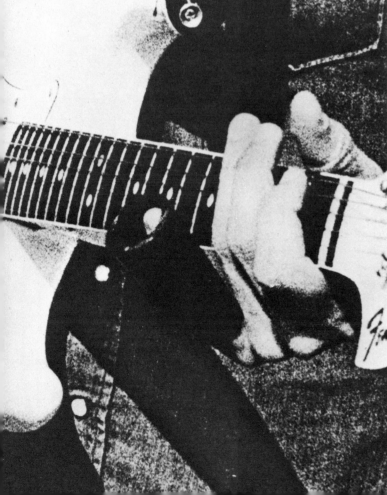

Foreword

The sound of the slide guitar is "in," popularized at long last by guitar players such as Mick Taylor, Johnny Winter, and Elvin Bishop, and by groups such as The Rolling Stones and The Doors.

Wherever music is played these days you're liable to hear the band do at least one slide number; and everywhere, pros and would-be pros are hastening to get down some "slide chops" against the day when they'll need to use that technique on the gig.

Considering the growing amount of interest in the style, it is surprising to realize that there exists virtually no literature whatever on the subject.

This present volume attempts to fill the need. In it, we have surveyed both today's electric lead styles, as well as some older, traditional styles of unaccompanied bottleneck playing. The emphasis throughout the book is on getting the player to express himself with a high degree of originality in each style, in a fairly short time.

Because good slide playing depends to such a large degree on the *kind* of sound produced (rather than on merely playing "correct" notes), the publishers felt that more was needed than just a standard instructional text.

That is why a record is included with this book. On the record, a group of fine, funky musicians (*see inside back cover*) cut a couple of jams: one blues and one Country & Western number. Slide guitar solos are featured on each. The solos are notated in such a way that even guitarists who do not read music can use them.

Text, diagrams and photos take the reader step-by-step through the solos, explaining how they were created and how the student can go about creating his own.

The last two numbers on the record are examples of unaccompanied bottleneck styles; and the same thorough-going analysis is applied to them.

Taking all things together, we believe that this SLIDE GUITAR INSTRUCTION MANUAL is the finest music instruction text ever produced; and that with its publication the day has come a little closer when the genuinely-interested music student can truly begin to believe in the ability of books to teach music.

Buck Mitchell III

Publisher
Green Note Publications

TABLE OF
TEXT

CONTENTS

TRANSCRIPTIONS

KEITH RICHARD

Introduction:

FUNDAMENTALS OF SLIDE GUITAR

In Front

We are going to reverse history somewhat and begin our study of slide guitar with examples of modern electric technique. Later on, we shall take up some traditional, unaccompanied forms of slide, or "bottleneck" playing. The material in this introductory section, however, applies equally to both styles of playing.

Basically, the idea behind all types of slide guitar playing is quite simple. Instead of stopping the strings with your fingers to produce pitches, you touch the strings with a "slide."

NORMAL
WAY OF
PLAYING

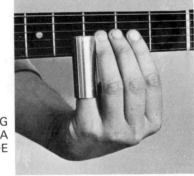
PLAYING
WITH A
SLIDE

Notice that the pictures above show the neck of a standard six-string guitar. All the guitar solos on the record included with this book, were played on this type of guitar, held in the conventional way (against the chest). This is the style that will primarily concern us throughout the book. (For more on this, see Appendix 4, *Other Slide Instruments & Techniques*, pp. 80-81.)

Types of Slides

Virtually anything can function as a slide. Most of the performers pictured in this book use some sort of metal tube. **Ry Cooder** (p. 25) and **Mississippi Fred McDowell** (p. 65), among many others, use the cut-off neck of a bottle. **Duane Allman** (p. 16) is shown using a small medicine bottle as a slide.

Below are a number of different objects commonly used as slides:

a) commercial slide which costs about $1.25; b) bottleneck; c) lipstick cover; d) and e) parts of toilet paper rollers; f) straight razor; g) pocket knife; and h) "steel" for pedal- or lap guitar.

Such other objects as small frozen juice cans and dashboard cigarette lighters (these primarily for lap playing) have also functioned as slides.

Besides experimenting with these objects, be on the lookout for other implements which, however unlikely-looking, might produce some unusual slide effects.

You can make your own bottleneck slide by scratching a line around the neck of a bottle with a glasscutter, heating the bottle in boiling water, and then plunging the scratched part of the bottle into ice-water. With a little pressure, the neck should crack right off. Sand the cut edge smooth.

Make sure, however, that the bottleneck you choose is flat, so that it will lie across the strings properly. The bottleneck shown to the right is a little too curved to lie evenly atop several adjacent strings at once.

Wearing the Slide

Most players wear the slide on the little finger. The fit is usually best there, and also allows chording with the other fingers. However, many players prefer to wear the slide on the ring finger. (See photos on pp. 16, 65, and col. 1, p. 80. In this last instance, notice how the little finger and middle finger help to hold the slide to the strings.)

Bottlenecks are usually worn on the finger with the cut side away from the hand:

If you want to use a knife (or razor) as a slide, here is one way you might hold it:

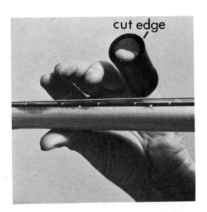

Or, you can rest the guitar on your lap and use the slide in this manner:

All these are only suggestions and the final criterion should be whatever is comfortable for you.

Slide Techniques

The slide should not be thought of merely as a substitute for the fingers. In several important ways slide technique differs greatly from conventional guitar technique.

1. Normally, you play the guitar by pressing the strings to the fingerboard with the fingers. However, when using the slide, *do not* press the strings to the fingerboard. Merely touch the slide to the string:

TOUCH
THE
STRINGS

DO NOT
PRESS
THEM

2. Place the slide directly *over* the fret wire, rather than behind it. This may take some getting used to, but it is absolutely essential for playing in tune:

SLIDE
DIRECTLY
OVER FRET

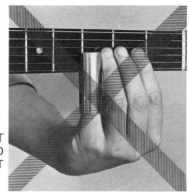

NOT
BEHIND
IT

SLIDE TECHNIQUES cont'd

3. Keep the slide level with the fingerboard:

LEVEL

NOT
TILTED

4. Try not to cover more strings than is necessary with the slide. For example, if you're playing mostly on the top two strings, you might let the slide cover three strings, but there is really no purpose in letting it cover four, five, or six strings. The more strings the slide touches, the more chance there is for scrapes, rattles and other uncontrolled sounds to occur:

COVER ONLY
WHAT YOU
NEED

NOT ALL
STRINGS
ALL THE
TIME

Keeping these four basic points in mind, let us begin working with the record.

BAND 1: Tuning Note

Tune your guitar to the note on Band 1. This note is a high E (found at fret XII) and is used in *Recorded Examples 1* and *2* coming up:

If you do not read either notes or tablature, now is the time to look at Appendix 1, *Tablature*, p. 76. (Note readers can also refer to the tablature if they have any doubt where a note is played.)

Once you have tuned your top string to this tuning note, tune the remaining strings by the method you normally use.

BAND 2 :: Recorded Ex.1

Play this band of the record and try to imitate the sound with your slide.

For the time being, use any picking technique that is comfortable and familiar to you. They all work well in this style. For example, **Keith Richards** (p. 6) is pictured playing with a flatpick; **Duane Allman** (p. 16) is picking with his fingers; while **Bukka White** (p. 56) uses both thumb- and fingerpicks.

The guitar solos on this record were picked with the fingers alone, but excellent results can be obtained with all kinds of combinations of flatpicks, fingers, and fingerpicks as well.

Below is *Recorded Example 1* in notation:

Notice the mark in front of the first note. This is a *slide mark* and indicates that you slide up into the note. Occasionally, a number appears above the slide mark. This number tells where to start the slide. In the example above, slide up *one fret* into the note.

> All notational symbols are explained in the text where they first occur. A complete list, for reference, can be found in Appendix 2, *Symbols Used in this Manual*, p. 77.

We will assume that you have played this recorded example somewhat to your satisfaction and are ready to go on.

BAND 3: Recorded Ex.2

Besides the high keening whine that characterizes the slide guitar sound, a *vibrato*, or tremulous, pulsating effect, is often heard. Listen for this on the second note of *Recorded Example 2*.

This sound is produced by keeping the slide on the string at as much of a fixed point as possible while *vibrating* the entire hand rapidly back and forth, somewhat in the following manner:

Violinists are traditionally seen using a great deal of vibrato. Vibrato not only produces a quavering effect, but also serves to lengthen the duration of a note, and is therefore particularly used with instruments like the violin and guitar, on which pitches rapidly decay.

Although a musical technique should never be used in an unvarying way, it is usually a good idea when playing slide style to use vibrato on any note you wish to sustain for a relatively long duration.

To test your vibrato technique, try to imitate Band 3 (*Recorded Example 2*). The notes are the same as in *Recorded Example 1*; but this time vibrate your hand on the second note to cause the wavering sound. Note the vibrato symbol used:

Now that you have some basic knowledge of how to use the slide and are satisfied that you can read the notation used in this book, let us move ahead into the actual music.

Part 1:

ELECTRIC LEAD-STYLE SLIDE GUITAR

Photo: Kevin/KLN Photos

DUANE ALLMAN

BAND 4: BLUES IN E

Listen to Band 4 a time or two to get a general idea of what is happening. Notice that this number consists of three choruses of lead guitar solo and three choruses of rhythm accompaniment to back you up when you feel ready to solo.

As you listen to the record, try to hear the chord changes. (If you feel you need some briefing in this, read up on blues form in Appendix 3, *Brief Analysis of the Blues*, pp. 78-79.)

After you have listened to Band 4 a time or two, try to copy some of the solo, using your ear alone. For the time being, pretend that you don't have the notation or analysis of this book to guide you. This type of ear-training will benefit you greatly.

On most records you are never entirely sure that you are copying all the notes you want exactly as they were played. On this record, however, you *can* know if you've copied correctly, since all the solos are completely notated and analysed.

Therefore, take advantage of this situation and try to copy the solo, or as much of it as you reasonably feel you can, on your own. The notation is always right at hand for you to look at if you get seriously stuck.

If at any point in your listening you feel that you would like to hear either the guitar or the background more clearly, you can bring out one or the other simply by adjusting the balance knob on your stereo record player.

This is a stereo recording and has the guitar on one track (coming from the right speaker), and the rhythm section on the other track (coming from the left speaker). Although this is a rather lopsided way of splitting instruments, it is a good way for our purposes, allowing us to "tune out" either the solo or the background as desired.

Another trick in record-copying is to slow the turntable speed of the record, making it easier to hear individual notes. To slow a 33 1/3 rpm record (such as the one that comes with this book), play it on a phonograph that can revolve at 16 rpm's.

Notice that the pitches, besides standing out, are lowered when you do this. Playing a 33 1/3 record at 16 lowers the notes a full octave; make sure to correct for this.

We will assume that you have tried copying some of this solo on your own and have been successful to one degree or another. Now let us work through it pretty much measure by measure.

The rhythm section begins with a couple of introductory measures. Then the guitar enters.

Below is a transcription of the first statement of the guitar solo, consisting of a pickup note and **measures 1-2**:

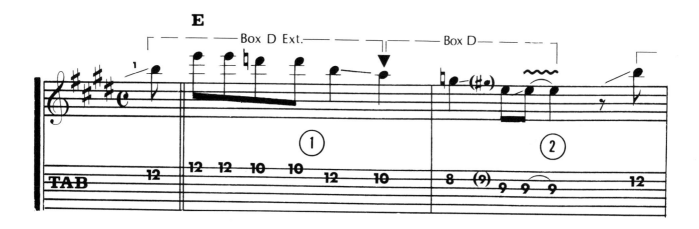

Circled numbers indicate measures. The slide and vibrato marks you should recognize from previous discussion. The wedge over the last note in **measure 1** indicates that the note was picked *after* it had been reached by sliding. If the wedge were omitted, you would merely slide into the note but not pick it.

The small notehead in parentheses in **measure 2** indicates that this pitch sounds as you move the slide between the first and third notes of the measure. (Absence of a wedge above this note means that the note is merely slid to but not picked.)

For the time being, disregard the brackets labeled Box D and Box D Extension; we will explain these later. The letter E above the brackets is a chord symbol.

Listen to the record, and notice the clean, crisp attack on most of the notes of this example. To achieve this, we must add a few new numbers to our list of slide techniques.

ſlide Techniqueſ CONT'D

5. At the same time that you are holding the slide to the strings, allow one or more fingers of the slide hand to rest lightly on the strings in the following manner:

DAMP
STRINGS

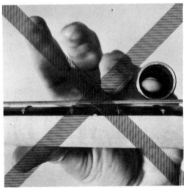

INSTEAD OF
LETTING THEM
RESOUND

Notice how much cleaner the sound becomes. Damping in this way cuts down string vibration and extraneous noise.

6. Also, damp with the fingers of the *pick hand* to cut out sustaining effect. Notice how in **measure 2**, even with the fingers of your slide hand damping the strings, the note on the second string (the small notehead in parentheses) resounds as you play the note on the third string. To keep this note from sustaining, damp the second string with a finger of the picking hand, somewhat in the following manner:

DAMPING
ON
ADJACENT
STRINGS

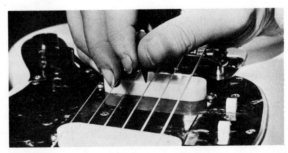

Here we have showed the middle finger of the pick hand coming up to damp the second string as the pick prepares to play the next note on the third string.

The same principle can be applied if you pick with your fingers. For example, pick the first note of **measure 2** with your thumb, damp that string with your index finger, then pick the next note with your thumb again.

Although these are methods of damping a string while picking notes on adjacent strings, the technique is basically the same if you want a crisp attack playing notes on the *same* string.

Play the first four notes of **measure 1**, picking and stopping each note in turn, using whatever pick hand damping method you find most comfortable. For example, if you use a flatpick, you might want to keep the middle finger real close to the top string in order to damp each note right after it is picked, as in the illustration below:

DAMPING
ON THE
SAME STRING

If you're picking with the thumb, you might want to keep your index finger in a similar damping position. A number of different string-damping arrangements are possible, each determined by the situation and your personal preference. What works in one situation may not work in another. Therefore, take the time to analyse each new situation and experiment with possible solutions. (Other possibilities include damping with the heel of the pick hand, or the side of the thumb.)

The sound you want to get is the first consideration, and any method you can come up with to achieve that sound is the "right" method.

Some of these techniques will take a little time to master, but you can console yourself in the meanwhile by remembering that these are very advanced techniques, used by some of the best players.

Keeping these points in mind, let's take a more complete look at Chorus 1, *Blues in E.*

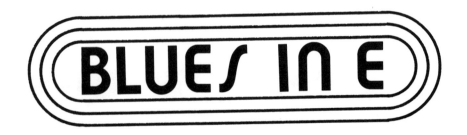

Cho. 1

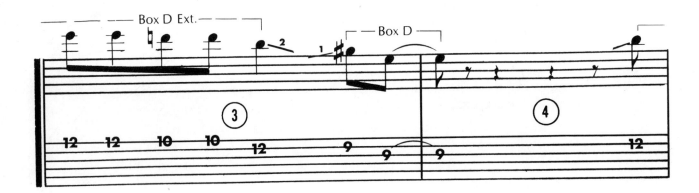
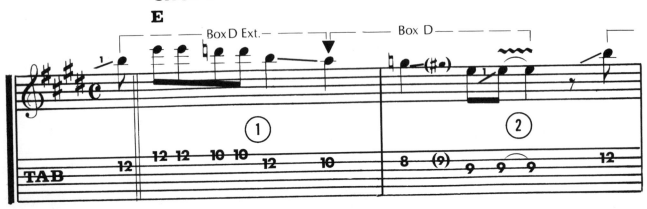

In **measures 3-4, 5-6,** and again in **7-8,** the statements are all variations of the original statement found in **measures 1-2.** This sort of repetition of even a simple phrase can be very effective in building interest in a solo: it involves you and the listener in a sort of musical "guessing game."

Look at the notes of this solo in relation to the chords played in the background. (This is discussed in Appendix 3, *Brief Analysis of the Blues,* pp. 78-79.) In **measures 1-4,** while the E chord is sounding, the first two statements each end on an E note and rest there for a relatively long duration.

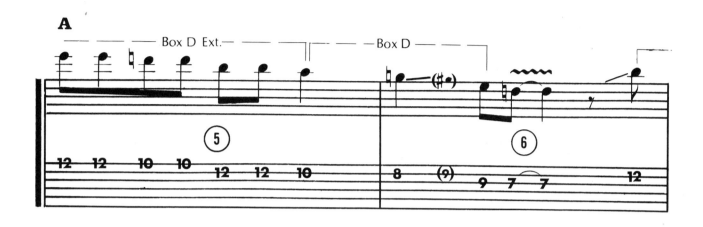

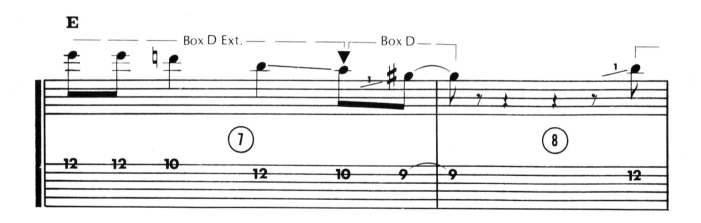

In **measure 5**, while the A chord is sounding, the note of longest duration is an A. In **measures 7-8**, the E chord is again sounding, and the melody comes to rest on a G♯, the third of an E chord, and a note which strongly implies the E chord sound.

BLUES IN E Cho. 1

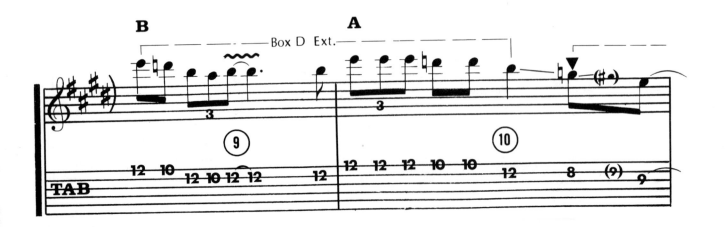

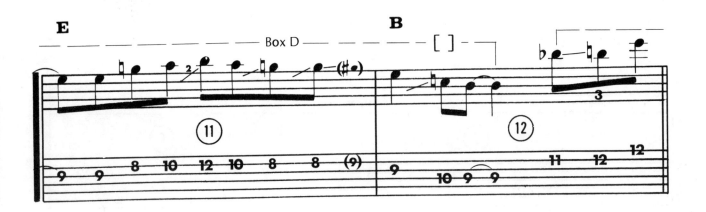

In **measure 9**, with the B chord sounding in the background, the note B is heavily stressed. **Measure 11** is another measure of E chord sound, and the phrase leading up to this measure (a final variation of the original statement) ends, appropriately enough, on the tonic.

In **measure 12**, the "turnaround" measure, a B chord sounds in the background, and melodically, the note B is held to stress the chord sound. The last beat of **measure 12** is a pickup leading to Chorus 2.

RY COODER

Improvi/ing Blue/ Guitar:
An On-Going Exegesis

So far our analysis of the preceding solo, helpful as it may ultimately prove to be, is a little too theoretical to really enable the student to begin serious improvisations on his own.

Instead, what seems to be needed by the great majority of guitarists, is some workable method of "visualizing" the fingerboard: of making sense, even at the beginning, of the maze of possibilities and complexities residing in the modern guitar.

To date, the only attempt at providing an immediately practical approach to guitar improvisation can be found in *Improvising Blues Guitar* (Green Note Publications, 1970).

In that book, a number of outstanding recorded blues solos were transcribed, then analysed as to where on the fingerboard they might have been played. From this analysis arose the concept of the Box System of guitar fingering, in which a few simple hand positions, or *boxes*, were seen to account for the great majority of all notes used in blues, rock, and certain types of jazz solos.

Essentially, a box is a small section of the fingerboard in which so-called "good" notes (notes characteristic of the idiom) can be easily played (that is, played without involving the fretting hand in awkward stretches or position-changes, and without placing too much responsibility on the relatively weak little finger).

Although these fingering considerations have little to do with the slide style of playing, nevertheless we can adopt parts of the Box System to fit our present needs. Refer now to the diagram on the following page:

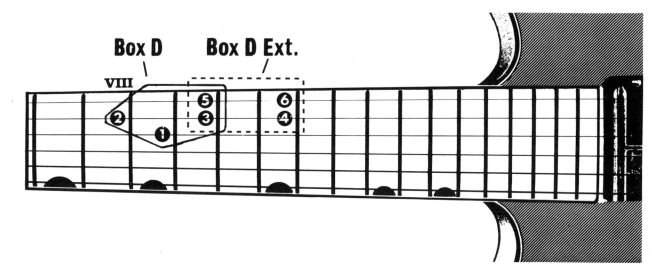

This diagram shows Box D and Box D Extension, two of the most widely-used positions in all of blues and rock playing.

> The name Box D derives from previous treatment of the Box System. It is in order to keep this method of fingering consistent from one Green Note publication to the next, that this seemingly strange terminology is being used.
>
> Also, we have decided to keep both positions shown above, under the common name, "Box D," rather than consider each a separate box. Once you have played these positions for a while, you will see how well they belong together.

Numbered dots above refer to the "good" notes we have mentioned. Without using the slide, and keeping the index finger positioned at fret VIII, play Box D and Box D Extension in the order the numbers indicate, using the following fingering:

> note 1 - middle finger
> 2 - index
> 3 - ring

Now slide the ring finger into note 4 and finish by playing:

> note 5 - index finger
> 6 - ring

IMPROVISING BLUES GUITAR cont'd

Here is how that looks in both music and tablature:

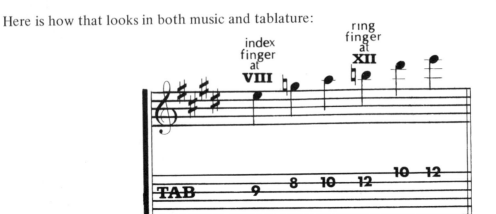

Play these notes a few times, again without the slide. Try to get the shape of the positions fixed in your mind. Perhaps you can begin to hear some characteristic blues and rock sounds from just these few notes.

Notice that notes 3 and 5 are either part of Box D or Box D Extension, depending upon which position your hand happens to be in at the moment.

Once you feel you have a fair idea of where the notes lie on the fingerboard, try finding them using the slide. Go back to Chorus 1, *Blues in E* (pp. 22-24) and this time pay particular attention to the brackets which indicate hand position.

In looking over this chorus you will probably notice that the tied note in **measure 6** as well as the note played at fret X in **measure 12** both lie outside Box D and Box D Extension.

For our present purposes, we are going to consider these two notes exceptions to our box rule. However, do not be discouraged at this early appearance of exceptions. Once the fundamental positions are learned, you will see that even exceptions become relatively easy to deal with.

After looking over Chorus 1 in terms of the positions used, play on the record, the rhythm background to *Blues in E*, and try improvising some slide ideas of your own, basing them around Box D and Box D Extension.

When you have done some of this, go on to Chorus 2, trying first to copy from the record, without using the transcription.

As you play, try also to remember the points of technique which we have already discussed and which will help you to achieve a good slide sound. These are summarized on the following page:

SUMMARY OF SLIDE TECHNIQUES

1. *Don't press strings to fingerboard with the slide.*
2. *Keep the slide directly over the fret wires for best intonation.*
3. *Keep the slide level over the fingerboard.*
4. *Keep the slide from covering more strings than is necessary.*
5. *Damp strings with fingers of slide hand to cut out extraneous noise.*
6. *Damp string using picking hand if crisp attack is desired.*
7. *Use vibrato on notes of relatively long duration.*

Additional factors that help make a clean slide sound are *string guage* and *string action.* Heavier strings and higher action (distance from string to fingerboard) both help to cut down extraneous string noise and give you a cleaner sound.

If you expect to play a lot of slide guitar, it would probably be wise to fit your guitar with relatively heavy guage strings (see inside back cover for specifications on the guitars used on this recording), and to raise the action on the guitar. If you have more than one guitar, you might want to fix one up in this way to keep especially for slide work.

Photo: George Hall

SHUGGIE OTIS

29

Cho. 2

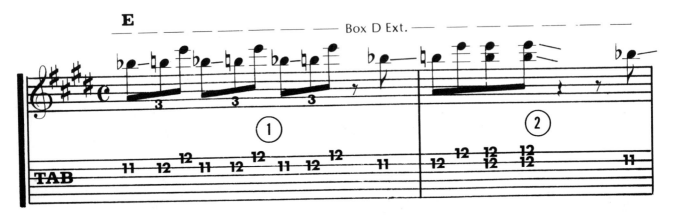

Measure 1 continues the phrase that closed Chorus 1. This is a very widely-used cliche, which still somehow manages to preserve its effectiveness. Notice how the rhythmic accent of this phrase is varied leading to **measure 2**. This varying of accent is repeated in **measures 2-3**. Often the most unexciting phrase can be suddenly enlivened by this sort of rhythmic variation.

Measure 2 shows the use of a *double-stop* (a two-note chord). Double-stops interspersed among single notes of a solo help create variety. Try to find other double-stops in Box D and Box D Extension which can be played easily when using the slide.

30

Record Band 4

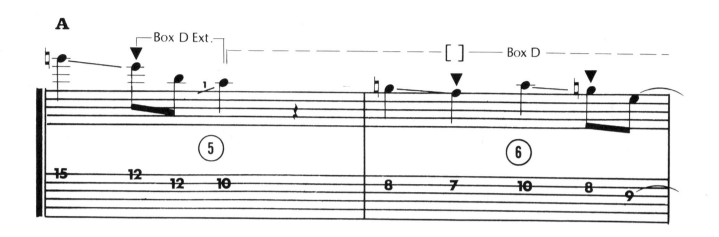

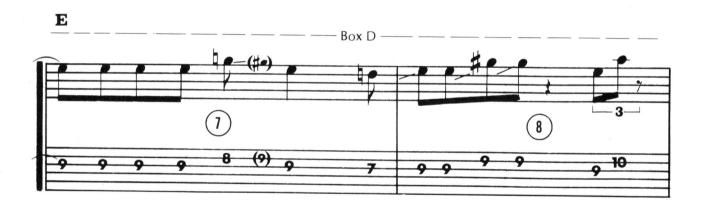

In **measure 4** and again in **measure 5**, the melody rises to a high G (at fret XV). We shall have more to say about this note in a moment when we finish looking at the remainder of this chorus.

The second note in **measure 6** is an "out-of-box" note. Experiment with the few exceptions we encounter, adding them to the safe box notes which you already know.

The last few notes in **measure 8** get very crisp attacks and you can be sure you've got your pick hand damping chops together if you can duplicate the sound of the record at this place.

BLUES IN E Cho. 2

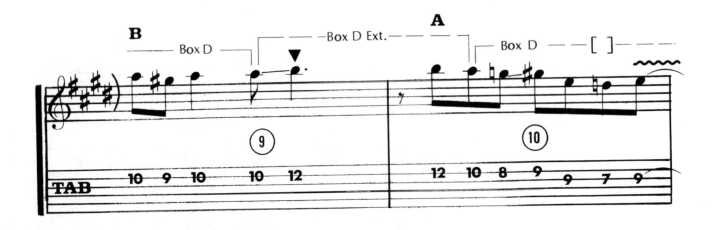

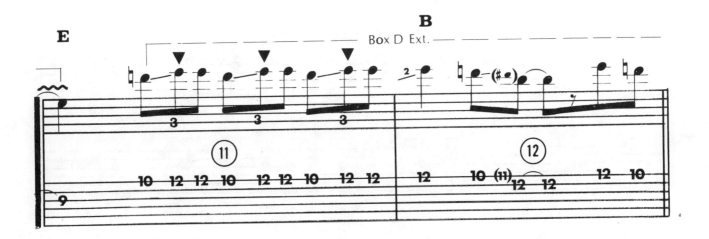

As you study and play this chorus, pay particular attention to the notes which are stressed in each measure. See how these important notes relate to the chord background.

MICK TAYLOR & THE ROLLING STONES at ALTAMONT, 1969

Improvising Blues Guitar CONT'D

Let us return now to the high G appearing in **measures 4-5**. Since this note lies outside both Box D and Box D Extension, we can either treat it as an exception to the box rule, or we can choose to find another box to put it in. Since there are a number of such "exceptions" found next, in Chorus 3, let us therefore introduce another widely-used position in the rock, blues, and jazz idioms—Box B:

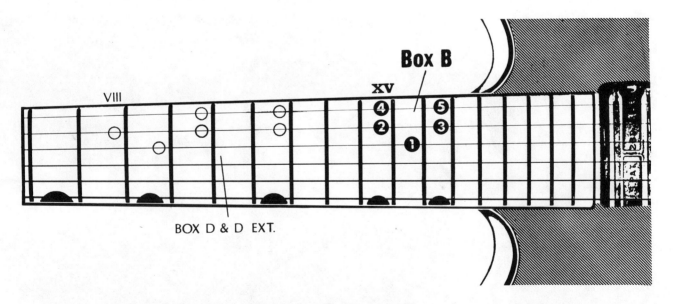

As you did with the other positions, play the notes of Box B a time or two without the slide to get the feel of the position. Keep the index finger at the fret indicated by the Roman numeral, and play the notes in the order the numbers indicate.

Octave Transposition

Besides playing Box B with the index finger at fret XV, as shown on the preceding page, you can also play Box B a full octave away, at fret III, and still remain in the same key. **Fingerboard 1**, this page, shows this.

You can do this with the other positions we have learned as well. In the key of E, you can play Box D both at fret VIII (which you should be getting somewhat familiar with by now), and also at fret XX (if you have a twenty-two fret guitar).

In this same key, however, Box D Extension can only be played in the high area if you happen to have a twenty-four fret instrument (and there are very few of these around). However, in another key, Box D and Box D Extension are more easily moved an octave up or down the neck.

You see that by such a simple maneuver you can extend your range on the guitar fingerboard considerably. **Fingerboard 2**, on this page, shows the few positions we have covered, each transposed an octave away wherever possible.

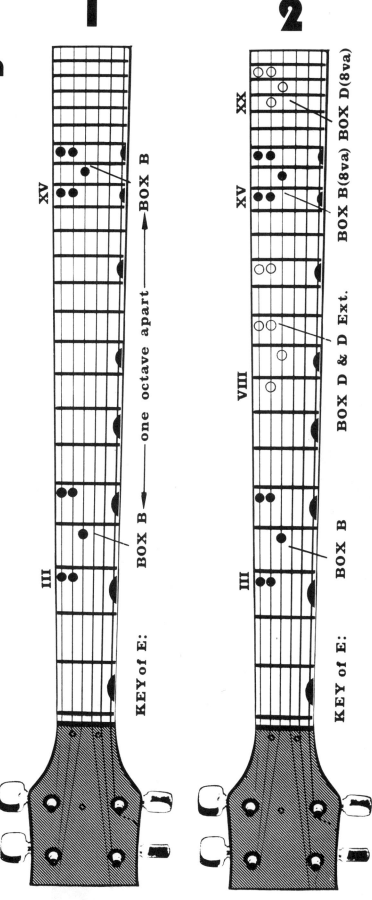

IMPROVISING BLUES GUITAR cont'd

In addition to octave transposition, each box and extension is fully movable up and down the fingerboard to accommodate changes in key. Following are tables showing the location of the three positions in all keys:

BOX D

Key	Index Finger At Fret No.:
A	I
B♭	II
B	III
C	IV
C♯(D♭)	V
D	VI
E♭	VII
E	VIII
F	IX
F♯(G♭)	X
G	XI
A♭	XII
A	XIII (=I)
etc.	

BOX D EXTENSION

Key	Ring Finger At Fret No.:
G	III
A♭	IV
A	V
B♭	VI
B	VII
C	VIII
C♯(D♭)	IX
D	X
E♭	XI
E	XII
F	XIII
F♯(G♭)	XIV
G	XV (=III)
etc.	

BOX B

Key	Index Finger At Fret No.:
D	I
E♭	II
E	III
F	IV
F♯(G♭)	V
G	VI
A♭	VII
A	VIII
B♭	IX
B	X
C	XI
C♯(D♭)	XII
D	XIII (=I)
etc.	

In the Box System, all **boxes** are located with the index finger; and all **extensions** are located by means of the ring finger.

Having played Box B a few times now, you should be able to see how the high G in **measures 4-5** of Chorus 2 fits into this position.

Noodle around with Box B for a while, without the slide, and try to fix the shape of the position in your mind. The longer you work with the boxes, the more familiar their shapes will become to you and the easier it will be for you to find the notes you want, even when using the slide.

Also experiment with the notes which lie between the safe notes in each box. You may not always like the results of such experimentation, but you will be using your ear and developing a style of your own at the same time.

Remember, these boxes will not automatically make you a great improvisor by themselves; however, treated as *frameworks* for musical invention, they will provide you with a solid and practical foundation for your trip toward becoming one.

When you feel fairly familiar with Box B, try to copy the next chorus, keeping Box B in mind when you come to passages involving high notes.

Photo: Joseph Sia

J.B. HUTTO

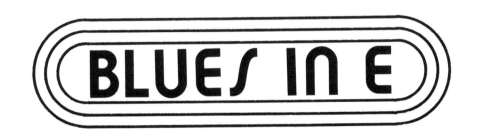

Cho. 3

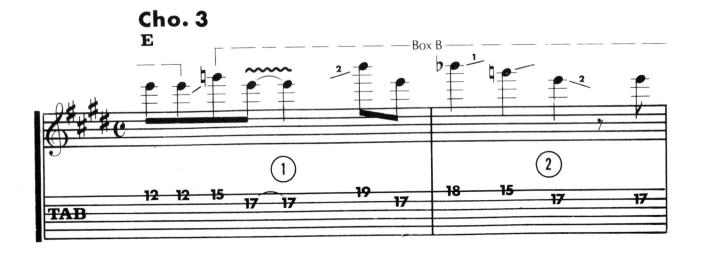

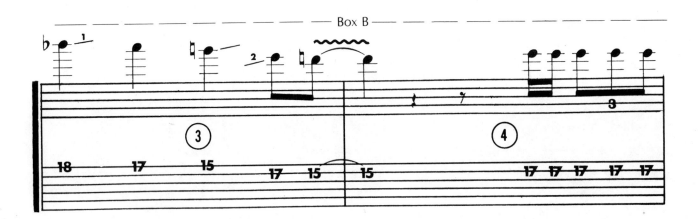

Measure 1 begins in Box D Extension, but the slide up to high G (fret XV) puts you in Box B. Instead of coming back down to the E played at fret XII, as we have been doing, stay in Box B and play the note E at fret XVII as shown.

If you look ahead at the rest of the solo, you can see the reason for staying in the high position here: many high notes, which make jumping back and forth between positions unnecessarily difficult.

Try to plan ahead in this way in your own improvising. Use the fact that you can play the same note in different places to your advantage.

38

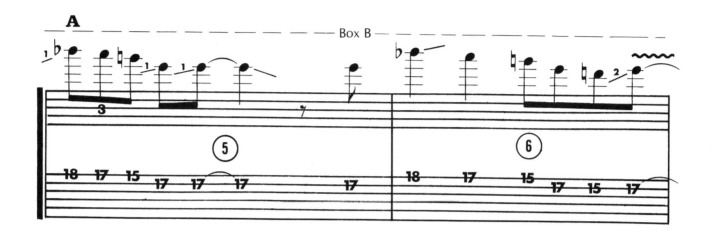

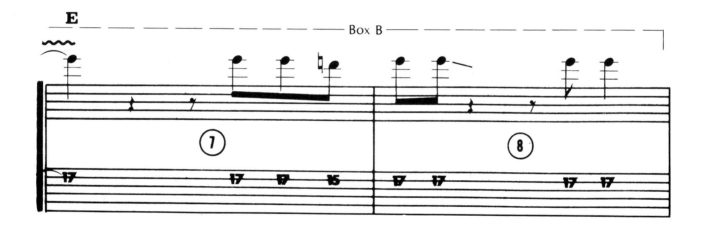

In **measure** 2 the high B (fret XVIII) is essentially part of Box B. Remember, the notes shown in the box diagrams are the most *characteristic* notes of each box, but other notes of the box can be played as well. In this case, if you were playing with your fingers, rather than with a slide, you could play high B with the little finger without moving your hand out of Box B.

Measures 3-8 are played entirely in Box B.

BLUES IN E Cho. 3

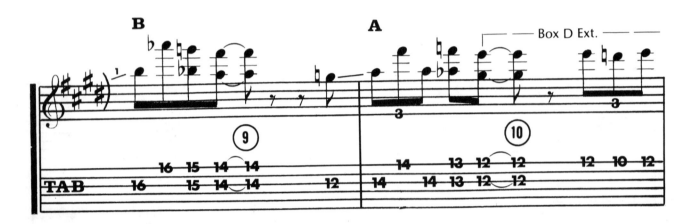

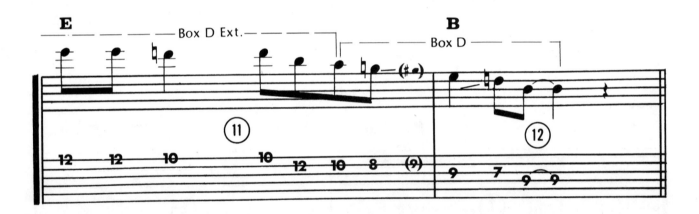

In **measures 9-10** we see some more examples of the use of double-stops. The first two notes of **measure 9**, as well as the first several notes of **measure 10**, can be thought of as double-stops even though the notes are picked individually. Let the first note of each group ring out and sustain while the second note is being picked; this will give the chord-like, double-stopped sound.

If you're using a flatpick, pick the top note of each double-stop with the middle finger, using the pick on the lower note. This flatpick-and-fingers technique is becoming more and more widely used by flatpickers, especially in such situations as the above, where notes have to be played either in quick alternation or simultaneously, on widely separated strings. Photos next page demonstrate this technique.

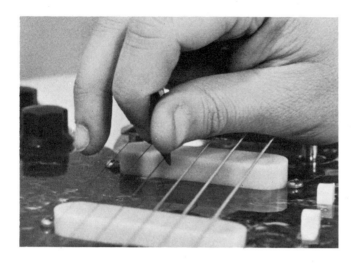

ALTERNATE PICKING
ON WIDELY-SEPARATED STRINGS

Flatpick plays low note (on third string), with middle finger in position to pick high note (on first string).

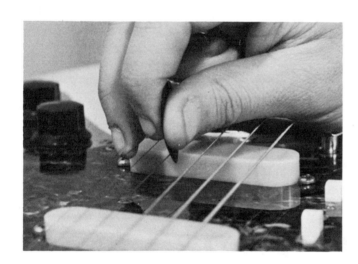

PICKING DOUBLE-STOPS
ON WIDELY-SEPARATED STRINGS

Flatpick and middle finger "pinch" first and third strings simultaneously.

In terms of position, a couple of the double-stops found in **measures 9-10** above, are technically part of Box B. However, taking **measures 9-10** as a whole, it is probably more meaningful to think of these double-stops as forming a series which simply descends by half-step to Box D Extension, where the series ends.

The rest of Chorus 3 is played in Box D Extension and needs no additional comment here.

RON WOOD

BAND 5: COUNTRY SLIDIN'

We leave the blues for a while and turn now to slide-style Country & Western lead guitar. The slide techniques involved here are the same used with the blues (holding the slide, damping the strings, and so on). However, we shall have some new things to say about methods of improvising in this style.

As you did with *Blues in E*, play Band 5 a time or two to get the sound of it in your ear. Then try to copy what you hear on the record on your guitar without looking at the music.

The longer you can put off peeking at the notation, the better training your ear will get, and the more meaningful the transcription will be when you eventually come to work with it.

We will assume that you have tried some copying. Following is Chorus 1, *Country Slidin'*. Check to see how close you came to figuring out the notes and positions just from listening to the record. For the time being, disregard the stars (★) that accompany the chord symbols; we will explain these later.

COUNTRY SLIDIN'

Cho.1

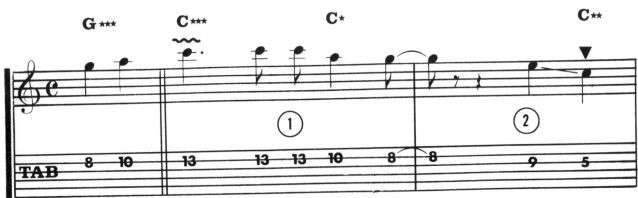

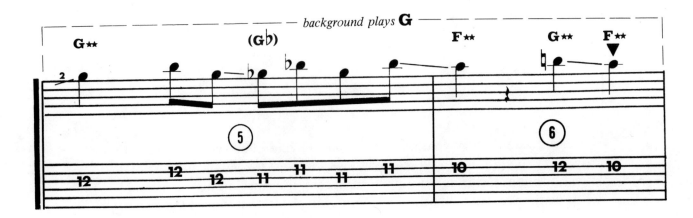

Record Band 5

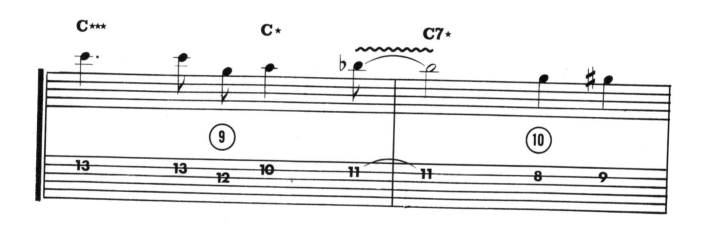

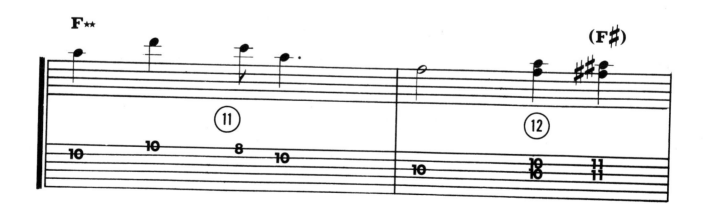

COUNTRY SLIDIN' Cho. 1

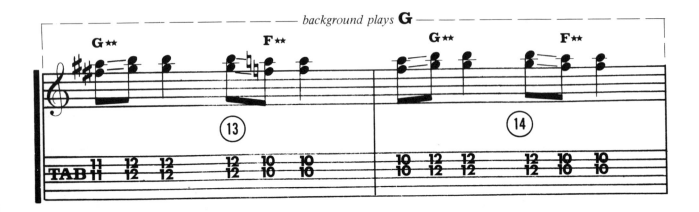

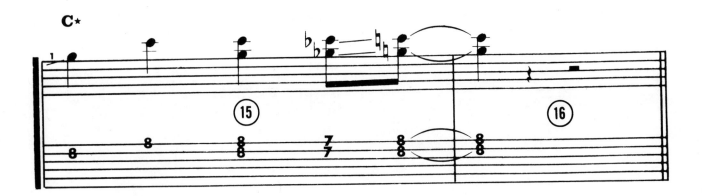

All slide techniques here are the same as those presented in the section on the blues; however, there is a chance that the positions used in the C&W tune might be unfamiliar to you. We shall discuss this now.

Improving Country & Western Lead Guitar

As different as they may sound, the blues and standard C&W tunes are actually similar to each other in several important respects. For example, both *Blues in E*, and *Country Slidin'* consist of just three chords and in each case the chords are the same: the I, IV, and V chords in the key. (*Blues in E*, as its title implies, is in the key of E and E, A, and B are the chords in that key. *Country Slidin'* is in the key of C, where the same chords are C, F, and G.)

However, although the tunes are similar in this way, you can see that the three chords are arranged differently in each case, and that *Country Slidin'* has more measures per chorus than does the blues:

STANDARD BLUES

I	∕.	∕.	∕.

IV	∕.	I	∕.

V	IV	I	I(V)

TYPICAL C&W

I	∕.	V	∕.

V	∕.	I	∕.

I	I 7	IV	∕.

V	∕.	I	∕.

IMPROVISING C & W LEAD GUITAR cont'd

For the reasons we just mentioned, you cannot simply base your improvisational ideas solely around the Box System, as you could with the blues.

If you want to test the truth of this statement, try playing in the box positions against the *Country Slidin'* rhythm background. (Remember to transpose the boxes into the key of C.)

Although you will get a good moment once in a while, your overall sound will be extremely limited, and you will miss getting the down-home flavor of the solo on this record. Some other basis, besides the Box System is needed for creating C&W lead guitar improvisations.

Although there are several possible approaches, the method we will use in this book is built around simple chord forms, of the kind that are familiar to most beginning guitarists.

Below you see a number of C, F, and G chords (the chords used in *Country Slidin'*) located at various places along the fingerboard. (The symbol ⌒ indicates a *barre*.)

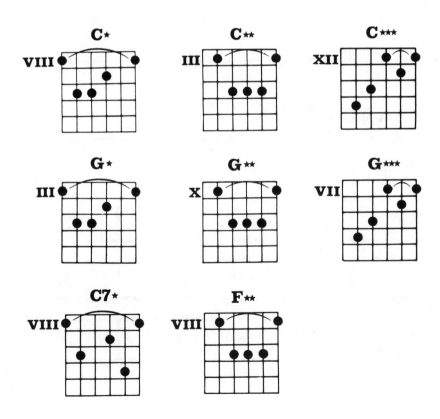

Since most electric slide work occurs on just the top three strings of the guitar, let us trim these relatively large chord-forms down to *triads* (three-note chords). Here is how the above chords look when played on only the top three strings:

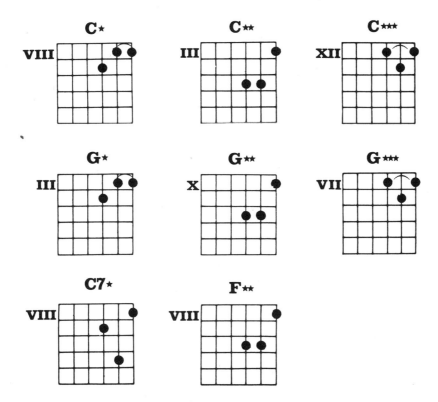

Now look back at Chorus 1 of *Country Slidin'*. Match the chord symbols and stars there with the chord diagrams on this page.

Without using the slide, hold down with the fretting hand, the three notes of each triad shown, and play the melody notes of Chorus 1. The purpose of this is to show you that all the notes of the solo can be played in these simple chord positions.

IMPROVING C & W LEAD GUITAR cont'd

Perhaps you noticed, in going back over this solo, that it is possible to play the first note of **measure 1** in C (★) (at fret VIII) instead of taking the trouble to switch to C (★★★).

Play the opening phrase both ways with the slide and note the difference in sound. One way involves playing on adjacent strings; the other way you keep to the same string.

Similarly, the last note of **measure 3** (the tied note), as well as the two notes in **measure 4** could have been played by staying in G (★), but the soloist, in order to get into a better position for the next part of the solo, decided to change to G (★★★).

In other words, use different forms of the same chord if the musical circumstances of the moment seem to demand it.

In **measures 5-6**, the notes strongly imply an alternation between an F and a G chord (with a half-step bridge connecting them in **measure 5**).

Since the subject of music theory lies pretty much outside the scope of this book, let us just say here that in the C&W idiom, this sort of solo switching between an F and G chord (while the background is playing a G chord) is best used just before going back to the tonic, or C chord (as in **measure 7**).

In **measure 15** there is a half-step slide into the C (★) chord, but no additional chord-form is needed to specify this.

Now that you have seen how this chord-form method of C&W lead guitar improvisation works, try a solo yourself (without the slide, for the time being). For the sake of simplicity (if the method is at all new to you), choose just one simple chord-form for each chord, such as:

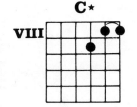
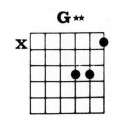
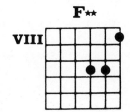
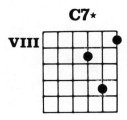

Play just that part of Band 5 which has the rhythm background, and try improvising around the position of each chord. Move your hand to the next appropriate chord-form whenever the background changes, and experiment with the different notes you can play while holding down the chord in each position.

If you have trouble hearing the background chords, follow the chord symbols on the notated solo, but use your own chord-forms and melodies.

When you can begin to visualize on the fingerboard the notes in each position you are using, then try to improvise using the slide. Remember, it takes a while to become familiar with the positions when you are not actually holding them down with your fingers, so do not expect to be proficient at this right away. However, through use they will eventually become familiar to you.

After you have worked with these positions for a while, go on to Chorus 2.

Just as you have done throughout this book so far, try to copy directly from the record before looking at the written music. When you are satisfied with your attempts to do this, then compare your results with the transcription which follows.

ELVIN BISHOP

COUNTRY SLIDIN'

Cho. 2

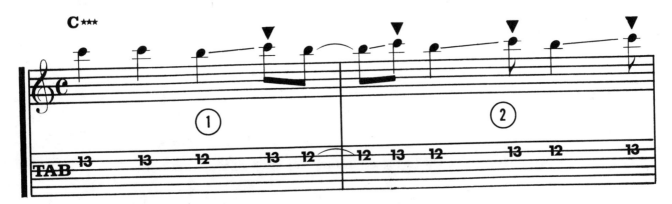

You remember we spoke earlier of the effectiveness of tasteful repetition. Notice the repetitive figures found throughout this chorus, especially in **measures 1-8**. After the more melodic phrases of Chorus 1, it is refreshing to find a bit of rhythmic repetition for contrast in Chorus 2.

We have also mentioned *chromatic* (half-step) motion a few times before. **Measures 1-8** show a great deal of this kind of melodic activity. You will find, if you look back, that Chorus 1 is relatively free of chromatic motion (except in those few measures involving double-stops). Therefore, it makes good sense (in terms of providing further contrast) to stress this kind of melodic motion in Chorus 2.

We also spoke earlier of rhythmic variation, of changing the accented note in a repeated figure. **Measures 1-2** and **4-6** are good examples of this. Much listener interest can be created by this simple device.

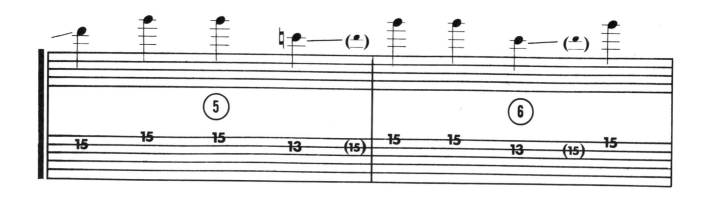

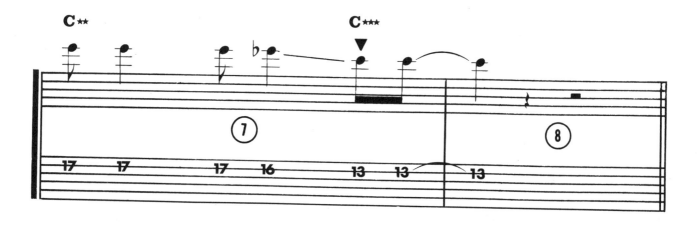

Beginning in **measure 4** and continuing through **measures 5-6** is a phrase characteristic of the C&W style which does not lie in one of the chord-forms we have discussed.

Actually, this is a variation on G (★★) and merely substitutes a higher note on the top string. Folk guitarists may recognize this chord-form as the so-called "long A" because it is usually used as an A chord with a half-barre at fret II. Here you see it as we are using it, transposed up almost a full octave to G.

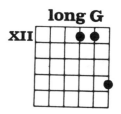

The C (★★) chord in **measure 7** is the same C (★★) chord we have already used, but this time transposed up one octave, from fret III to fret XV.

COUNTRY SLIDIN' Cho. 2

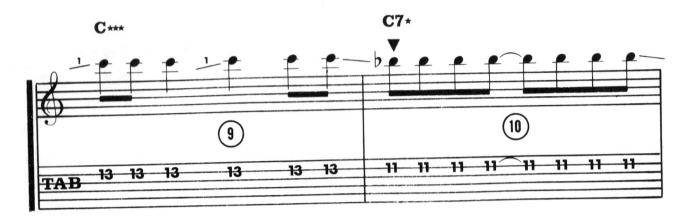

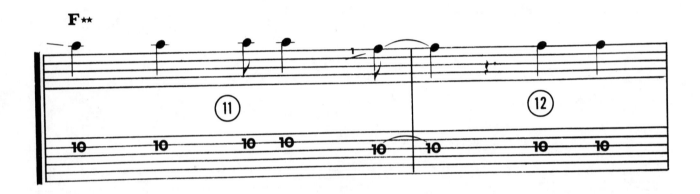

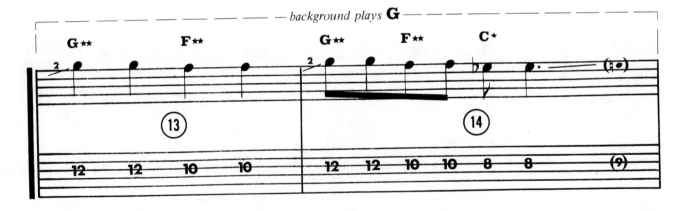

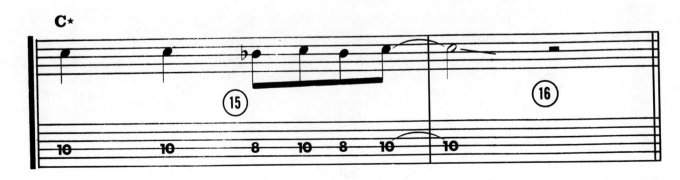

In **measures 14-16** a hint of the blues briefly emerges, and these last measures of our C&W solo could have been played in Box D Extension and Box D instead of in the C (★) chord-form position, where it actually was played.

This type of situation simply points up the fact that methods and systems often merge and overlap, and that the best course the student can take in such a case is to make use of both viewpoints to aid him in his musical development.

Part I Conclusion...

We have now come to the end of this present discussion of electric lead-style slide guitar. Work with the positions and techniques shown, and above all experiment on your own, and spend a good deal of time copying from records that you like.

Following is a short list of current, easily-obtainable records which feature examples of fine electric slide guitar playing:

ELECTRIC SLIDE DISCOGRAPHY

ELMORE JAMES
"To Know A Man"
Blue Horizon 7-66230 (stereo)
Slide artistry of a near-legend. This two-record set includes, interestingly enough, several takes of a number of tunes, and shows the gradual buildup and improvement of the final recorded version.

EARL HOOKER
"Hooker & Steve"
*Arhoolie 1051 (stereo)
Bluesman Earl Hooker backed by keyboardman Steve Miller, of The Elvin Bishop Group. A great record to copy slide licks from.

JB HUTTO
"JB Hutto & The Hawks"
*Testament Records T-2213 (stereo)
Chicago slide by a disciple of Elmore James.

JOHN LITTLEJOHN
"Chicago Blues Stars"
*Arhoolie 1043 (stereo)
Fine urban blues guitarist in the tradition of BB and Albert King, who uses the slide as well.

DUANE ALLMAN
"Eat A Peach"
Capricorn 2CP 0102 (stereo)
Last recordings by Duane Allman, this two-record set features standout slide solos by him on several tracks.

MICK TAYLOR & KEITH RICHARDS
"Sticky Fingers"
Rolling Stones 712190-MO (stereo)
Slide guitar solos and backing on many tracks. If you get the chance, compare the Stones' version of "You Got To Move" (written by Fred McDowell) with Fred's own version (listed in the Traditional Discography, p. 73).

SAM MITCHELL (Rod Stewart, vocal)
"Every Picture Tells A Story"
Mercury SRM 1-609 (stereo)
Typical of many new rock and pop releases in its widespread use of slide guitar—both acoustic and electric styles, as well as pedal steel guitar.

JOHNNY WINTER
"About Blues"
Janus JLS-3008
One electric slide track.
"Johnny Winter"
Columbia CS 9826 (stereo)
Two acoustic slide tracks on this, his first album.

SHUGGIE OTIS
"Here Comes Shuggie Otis"
Epic BN 26511 (stereo)
One track of acoustic slide guitar showcased against a big band sound.

ROBBIE KRIEGER (& The Doors)
"Other Voices"
Elektra EKS 75017 (stereo)
Slide guitar on two tracks.

*Addresses of the smaller, independent record companies are listed on p. 73.

Part 2:

TRADITIONAL-STYLE SLIDE GUITAR

Photo: Jim Marshall

BUKKA WHITE

Open Tunings

Up to now all our recorded examples of slide guitar have been played using the standard guitar tuning,

$$E - A - D - G - B - E$$

However, although this tuning is widely used in lead-playing, other, so-called "open" tunings lend themselves more readily to an unaccompanied style of slide playing.

Essentially, an open tuning is one where all open, or unfretted strings, when strummed, give the sound of a simple chord. For example, if we were to take a standard-tuned guitar and raise the fourth and fifth strings one whole step, the guitar would then be tuned to an "open" E— (minor) chord:

$$E - \textcircled{B} - \textcircled{E} - G - B - E$$

Circled notes are those changed from the standard tuning. To raise the fourth string one whole step, tune this string so that it sounds an octave below the open first string. To raise the fifth string one whole step, tune this string so that it sounds an octave below the open second string.

If all open strings produce an E— chord (as in our example above), you can easily see that a slide placed along all the strings in fret I would produce an F— chord, across fret II an F♯ — chord, and so on.

It is this limitation of the slide (in being able to play only chords which lie entirely in one fret) that has given rise to the practice of open tunings.

There are any number of possible open tunings. The E— tuning we have showed above was called "cross-note" tuning by **Skip James**.

By raising the third string as well as the fourth and fifth strings, **Son House** came up with an E (major) tuning, which he calls "Cross Spanish" tuning:

$$E - \textcircled{B} - \textcircled{E} - \textcircled{G\sharp} - B - E$$

SON HOUSE

Another "raised string" tuning which produces some unusual banjo-like effects, is the so-called "high G" tuning. Here, the open third string, normally tuned to middle G, is instead tuned to G a full octave higher:

MIDDLE G

HIGH G

Since you can't tune a normal guitar G string this high without breaking it, the thing to do is to use a banjo A string for this purpose.

OPEN TUNINGS cont'd

Besides raising strings, you can lower them to achieve open tunings. Following are a couple of widely-used open tunings obtained by lowering the strings:

(D) – A – D – (F♯) –(A)–(D)   (D tuning)

(D)–(G)– D – G – B –(D)   (G tuning)

In addition to these, an almost infinite variety of tunings are possible. Obviously, you will not be able to master the possibilities of all tunings, but if you are interested in open tunings at all, you might want to find one or two that you like and stay with them till you learn them well.

In all this talk about experimenting with different tunings, one word of caution should be included: be careful not to tune your strings too high, especially if you are using heavy guage strings, or are changing the tunings on a 12-string guitar. Too much string tension can easily cause neck warpage or, in some cases, even pull the bridge from the top of the guitar, often with disastrous results.

One way of getting certain "raised note" tunings without risking additional string tension is to first lower the strings and then use a *capo* (a slide-like device which clamps to the fingerboard) to raise them:

OPEN D TUNING . . . . becomes . . . . OPEN E TUNING

with capo at fret II

Now that you have some idea of how certain sounds are achieved in traditional slide playing, let us look at the recorded solos.

BAND 6: LOW-DOWN D

As you did with Bands 4 and 5, listen to this band a few times and try to figure out how the tune might be played. A hint: tune your sixth (thickest) string down to low D. This note should sound one octave lower than the D on the open fourth string.

Essentially, this solo functions as a transition between the lead style we have been working with and older styles of playing. It is a blues, but a 16-bar blues (with a 4-bar "tag" ending) rather than the 12-bar form which we worked with earlier.

Throughout the entire tune, the thumb keeps up a steady bass line, alternating between the open sixth and fourth strings, while the index and middle fingers pick out the melody on the top three strings.

Unless you are familiar with this style of playing you will probably have to practice a bit coordinating the movement of your thumb with that of your other fingers. As a way of getting into this tune, spend some time getting the thumb (T) to play the bass figure below so that it becomes almost automatic:

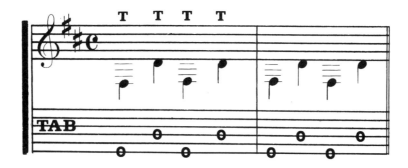

Another thing to be aware of in playing this solo is to keep your slide from touching the fourth string and thus interfering with the steady bass pattern. It is essential that this string be kept open, and you will probably have to work on this a while before it becomes entirely natural.

Now that you have some idea of what is in this number, you might want to exercise your ear a little by trying to copy the melody played on the top strings. When you have done this to your satisfaction, check your work against the transcription that follows.

LOW-DOWN D

6th string to D

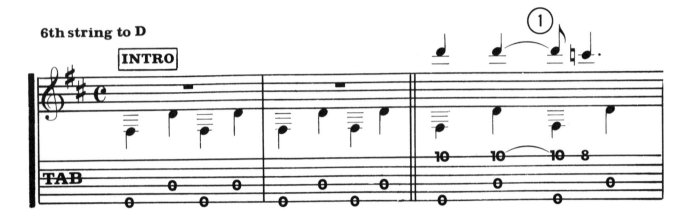

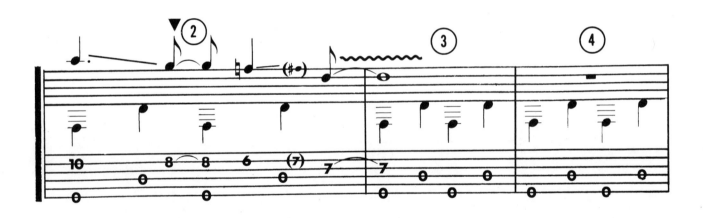

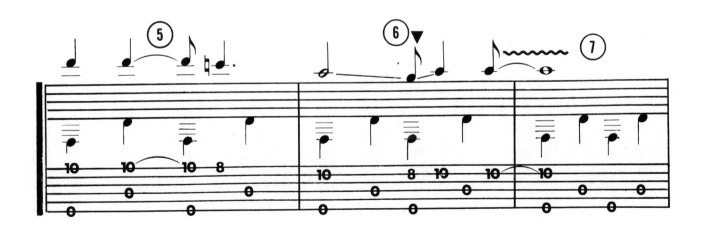

Record Band 6

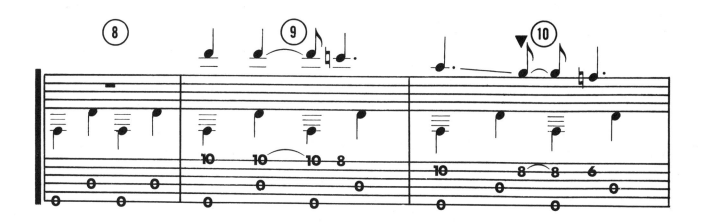

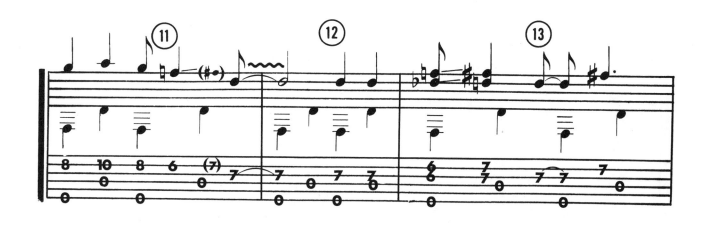

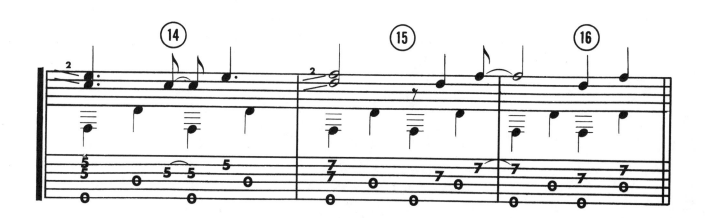

LOW-DOWN D

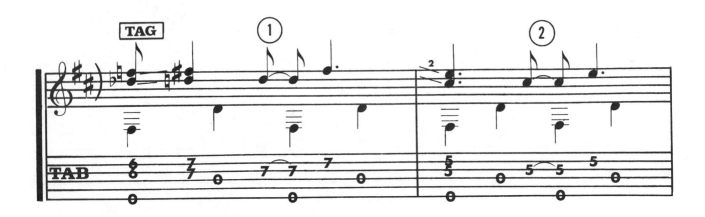

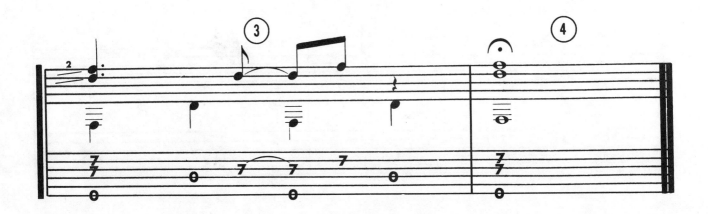

Notice the use of syncopation throughout the solo: how the melody notes on the treble strings are played "off-the-beat" in contrast to the steady "on-the-beat" rhythm of the bass line.

Notice too that the entire melody is built around Box D and Box D Extension, with the lone exception of the double-stopped figure found in **measure 14** and in **measure 2** of the tag ending.

We have encountered these notes before, in *Blues in E*, and though they are exceptions to our box rule at this time, you will find them used a great deal in slide playing.

64

After you have gained some facility with this finger-style tune, try making up some solos of this type on your own.

You might begin with a bass pattern. It can be something quite simple. For example, in standard tuning, in the key of E, try playing a steady, recurring "drone" note on the sixth string with your thumb. Then pick out some notes on the top strings, using the slide, as in the following example:

FRED McDOWELL & MIKE RUSSO

ELVIN BISHOP

BAND 7: OPEN-G RAG

This next recorded selection is a full-fledged example of traditional bottle-neck style, with heavy emphasis on a full, chordal sound. Although it is a blues of the 12-bar variety, it begins, strangely enough, on the IV chord (a C chord in the key of G), and does not begin to look like a true blues until **measure 7**:

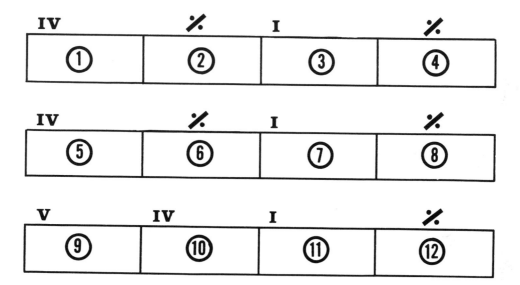

Listen to the recording a few times and see if you can figure out on your guitar what is happening. Complex as the piece may sound, it is really quite easy to play for the most part. Try learning some of it before looking at the notation which follows.

As its title implies, this number is in G tuning:

Ⓓ–Ⓖ– D – G – B –Ⓓ

For most players the easiest right hand technique to use involves plucking the strings with the thumb and fingers.

Cho. 1

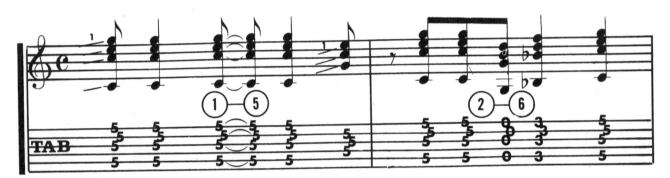

Keep the slide over all five strings where necessary. In **measures 3-4** and **7-8**, for example, you can see that it is not necessary.

Notice the repeat sign at the end of **measure 4**. This sign tells you to go back to the beginning and repeat all the measures up to the repeat sign before going on.

Although this means that **measures 5-8** are to be played just like **measures 1-4**, you may notice, in listening to the record, that slight differences do exist between the two sections, most noticeably on the last upbeat of **measures 1/5** and **4/8**.

Record Band 7

These differences are not especially important here. What is important in these particular places is the rhythmic aspect of the notes played, rather than their actual pitches (providing, of course, that the notes involved are proper to the chord of the moment).

Therefore, one time the performer may play a chord, the next time just one note of that chord, the third time he may perhaps decide to rhythmically *slap* the strings (as in **measure 9**).

In such cases it is less important to try to copy the exact notes produced, than to get the general spirit of the playing.

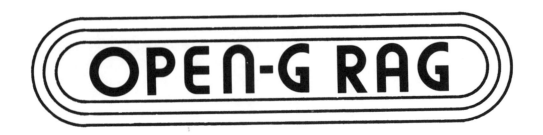

Cho.2

This chorus is much the same as Chorus 1, with a few variations.

In both choruses use vibrato at every opportunity to get the sound of the record. Because so much vibrato is used in this tune, the symbol indicating vibrato has been entirely omitted.

Record Band 7

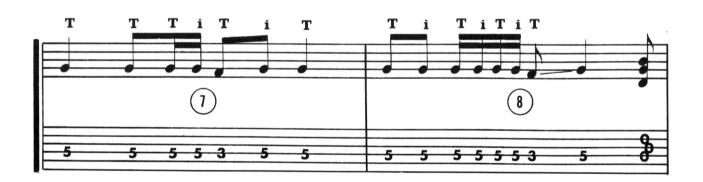

Pick the single-string passages in **measures 7-8** with a rapid alternation of the thumb and index finger as shown. (T = thumb; i = index finger.)

OPEN-G RAG Cho.2

Measure 11 contains a typical blues cliche, one which would be good to learn in a variety of keys and perhaps in a couple of favorite tunings, if you expect to play the blues much.

Fret this passage with the fingers of the fretting hand rather than with the slide, keeping the middle finger on the sixth string and the ring finger on the fourth string as you descend. (Right hand fingering is indicated by T, m (middle finger), i.)

The ending chords in **measure 12**, reveal the Hawaiian sound traditionally associated with slide guitar.

72

Now that you have played through this tune, experiment with it. Change the tempo, for example, and explore other areas of the fingerboard.

Try changing the tuning. Lower the B string one half-step, for example, to:

$$\textcircled{D} - \textcircled{G} - D - G - \textcircled{B\flat} - \textcircled{D}$$

which is an open G— chord, and see what happens.

Do not worry about playing in a particular form, or about having to make certain chord changes at specified places. Play what sounds good to your ear and let the writers of instruction manuals try to figure out what you have done.

Above all, listen a great deal to records and try to learn from them. The following discography lists a number of records which feature traditional-style slide guitar playing.

TRADITIONAL SLIDE DISCOGRAPHY

ROBERT JOHNSON
"King of the Delta Blues Singers"
Columbia CL 1654
Excellent record by the legendary figure to whom so many guitarists—from Elmore James to Eric Clapton—acknowledge their debt.

FRED MCDOWELL
"Mississippi Delta Blues"
*Arhoolie F 1021

"Fred McDowell—Vol. 2"
*Arhoolie F 1027

This last includes "You Got To Move," featured on the Rolling Stones' "Sticky Fingers" album.

BUKKA WHITE
"Sky Songs" (Vol. II)
*Arhoolie F 1020

"At Home With Friends"
*Asp ASP 1
Split record with slideman Furry Lewis.

FURRY LEWIS
"Back On My Feet Again"
Prestige PR 7810

"Live At The Gaslight"
Ampex A 10140

SON HOUSE
"Father of the Folk Blues"
Columbia CS-9217

*Arhoolie Records
P. O. Box 9195
Berkeley, Ca. 94719

*Testament Records
577 Levering Ave.
Los Angeles, Ca. 90024

*Asp Records
10123 66th St.
Seattle, Wash. 98178

FURRY LEWIS

APPENDICES

APPENDIX I:
Tablature

Below the conventional treble-clef staff is a special six-line staff on which the word TAB appears at the beginning of each transcribed solo chorus:

Each line of the TAB staff corresponds to a string on the guitar: topmost line to the high E (thinnest) string; second line to the B string, and so on, down to the bottommost line which corresponds to the low E (thickest) string:

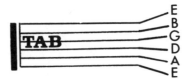

Numbers appearing on the lines of the TAB staff correspond to notes in the treble-clef staff and indicate at which fret a particular string is either to be pressed with the finger or touched with the slide:

TAB shows only where the notes are located on the guitar. The time-value of the notes must be found in the treble-clef staff, along with expression marks and other symbols.

Special fingering instructions appear throughout the text wherever the need for them arises.

APPENDIX 2:
Symbols Used in this Manual

1

Slide up to a particular note. (Numbers accompanying all slide marks indicate distance of slide, e. g., *one*-fret slide, *two*-fret slide, etc.)

2

Slide up to no particular note.

3

Slide down to a particular note.

4

Slide down to no particular note.

5

Wedge: note picked.

6

Small note head: this note sounds as you pass from the first note to the third note, but is not picked.

7

Vibrato.

8

Roman numeral: indicates fret at which note is located.

9

Note played on open string.

10

Note (or chord) played with string(s) damped. In cases like these, pitch is of secondary importance: rhythmic attack is primarily emphasized.

11

Hold/sustain.

12
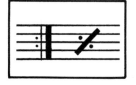

Repeat signs.

APPENDIX 3:
Brief Analysis of the Blues

Since so much has been written elsewhere about the blues and blues form, our treatment of the subject here will be brief.

Chords

Standard blues length is 12 measures, divided among only three chords in the following manner:

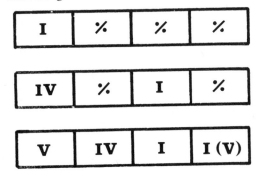

Roman numerals indicate chords. For example, in the key of C, the I chord (also called the *tonic* chord) is a C chord; the IV chord is F (arrived at by counting up four letters alphabetically from C); the V chord is G. The table below lists the I, IV, and V chords in the most-used keys:

KEY	I	IV	V
C	C	F	G
D	D	G	A
Eb	Eb	Ab	Bb
E	E	A	B
F	F	Bb	C
G	G	C	D
Ab	Ab	Db	Eb
A	A	D	E
Bb	Bb	Eb	F
B	B	E	F#

In ending, play the I chord in the last measure. However, if you want to play another *chorus* of the blues (12-bar segment), change instead to the V chord in the last measure. This so-called "turn-around" chord takes you back to the beginning.

Melody

What notes to use in improvising blues is treated throughout the analysis of the recorded material in this book, and specifically on pp. 26-29 and 34-37. Here we can briefly say that any *chord note* sounds good. For example, in the key of E, if the background plays an E (I) chord:

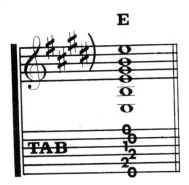

any note of that chord, played in any order (as well as in any octave) sounds good as a melody note:

In addition to chord notes, it is part of the peculiar nature of the blues which allows you to play certain *flatted* notes against the standard chords with good results. In fact it is this "flatted" quality which gives the blues much of its characteristic sound. For example, this *flatted third* in the key of E sounds fine played against the standard E chord, with its *major third*:

Below is a blues scale made up of chord notes, flatted notes, and scale notes in the key of E:

flatted third
(lowered ½-step
from major third)

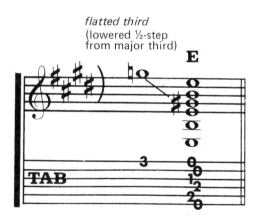

The notes of this scale all sound "good" when played against a standard blues progression. Although you can use many more than just these five notes when improvising, this simple scale provides the basis of much blues, rock, and jazz improvisation. We shall show examples of this scale at work in our analysis of the recorded blues material.

APPENDIX 4:
Other Slide Instruments & Techniques

The recorded guitar solos used in this book were played on standard six-string guitars (both electric and acoustic) held in the normal manner.

However, there are several other ways of playing slide guitar, and several distinct types of instruments commonly associated with the slide sound which should be mentioned.

National Steel Guitars and Dobros

Both of these are brand names for a type of acoustic guitar which uses a metal "loudspeaker," or *resonator* (built into the top of the guitar) to increase the guitar's volume of sound.

Examples of National steel guitars can be found on pp. **6, 56,** and **59.** The picture below, taken at the 1970 Ann Arbor Blues Festival, shows an unidentified performer with a beautiful example of another resonator-type guitar:

Photo: Joseph Sia

Lap Guitars

Below you see **BUKKA WHITE,** one of **B.B. KING'S** early influences, playing his National steel in the lap position:

Photo: Lynn Adler/Optic Nerve

Compare this photograph of Bukka with the one on p. **56.** Note the different slides used.

The guitar shown below (played by **GEORGE CUMMINGS**, of **DR. HOOK & THE MEDICINE SHOW**) was made especially for lap playing:

Photo: Ron Scherl

Instruments like these come in both acoustic as well as electrically amplifiable models, and are usually fitted with either six or eight strings.

Pedal Steel Guitars

Below is **JERRY GARCIA**, seated at a full-fledged electric pedal steel guitar. This model features two fingerboards, each equipped with ten strings (some models employ as many as three terraced fingerboards), and foot-pedals for changing tunings while playing:

Photo: Robert Altman/Optic Nerve

NOTE: Since the first printing of SLIDE GUITAR, we have received a number of letters asking for sources of manufactured slides. The following list of manufacturers makes no claim to being complete, but simply represents those companies we managed to locate in the short interval that occurred between printings. All have agreed to respond to individual orders.

Imagineering Enterprises, 3017 E. Calhoun Blvd., Minneapolis, Minn. 55408
Jan-Mar Industries, 201 W. 49th St., New York, N. Y. 10019
Lightning Music Supplies, Box M-104, Bay Shore, N. Y. 11706
Super Star Products, 16209 Mack Ave., Detroit, Mich. 48224

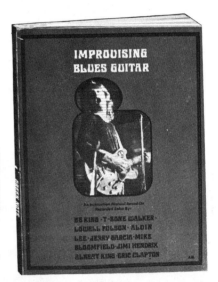